The Magic School Bus

Inside the Earth

The Magic School Bus
Inside the Earth

By Joanna Cole

Illustrated by Bruce Degen

Scholastic Inc.

New York · Toronto · London · Auckland · Sydney
Mexico City · New Delhi · Hong Kong · Buenos Aires

*The author and illustrator wish to thank Dr. George E. Harlow,
Associate Curator, Department of Mineral Sciences
at The American Museum of Natural History,
for his assistance in preparing this book.*

*The author would also like to thank Dr. Peter Bower,
Professor of Geology at Barnard College,
for his helpful consultation.*

ISBN-13: 978-0-590-40760-1
ISBN-10: 0-590-40760-0

Text copyright © 1987 by Joanna Cole.
Illustrations copyright © 1987 by Bruce Degen. Cover illustration © 1997 by Bruce Degen.
All rights reserved. Published by Scholastic Inc.

SCHOLASTIC, THE MAGIC SCHOOL BUS, and associated logos are trademarks
and/or registered trademarks of Scholastic Inc.

25 26   10 11 12 13

Printed in the U.S.A.   40

The illustrator used pen and ink, watercolor, color pencil,
and gouache for the paintings in this book.

To Michael Stone

—J.C.

To Maxwell "Mickey" Cohen and
Henry "Hank" Silverstein, who
have rocks in their heads.

—B.D.

In Ms. Frizzle's class,
we had been learning about
animals' homes
for almost a month.
We were pretty tired of it.
So everyone was happy
when Ms. Frizzle announced,
"Today we start something new."

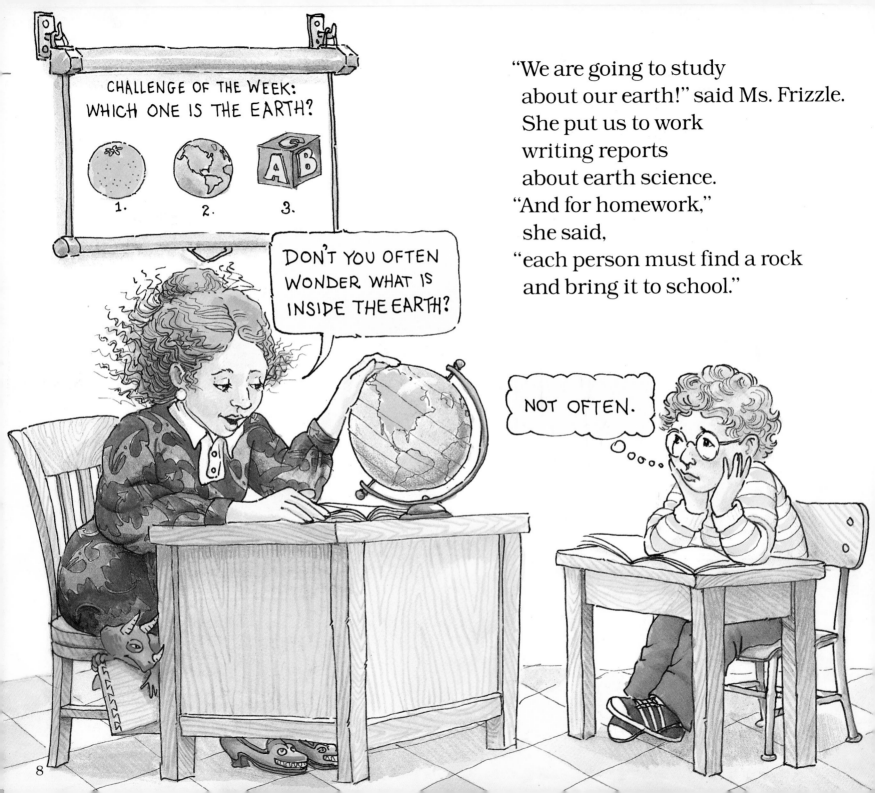

"We are going to study
  about our earth!" said Ms. Frizzle.
 She put us to work
  writing reports
  about earth science.
"And for homework,"
  she said,
"each person must find a rock
  and bring it to school."

But the next day, almost everyone had some excuse.

I COULDN'T FIND ANY ROCKS.

I FOUND ONE, BUT MY DOG ATE IT.

YOUR DOG ATE A ROCK?

WHERE DO ROCKS COME FROM? by Wanda

Most of the solid part of the earth is made of great masses of rock.

The small rocks that we collect are just pieces that broke off from these huge masses.

9

Only four people
had done the homework.
And Phil was the only one
who had found a real rock.

You never know
what will happen
on a trip with Ms. Frizzle.
Her new dress
was a trip in itself.
At first the old school bus
wouldn't start.
But finally we were on our way.

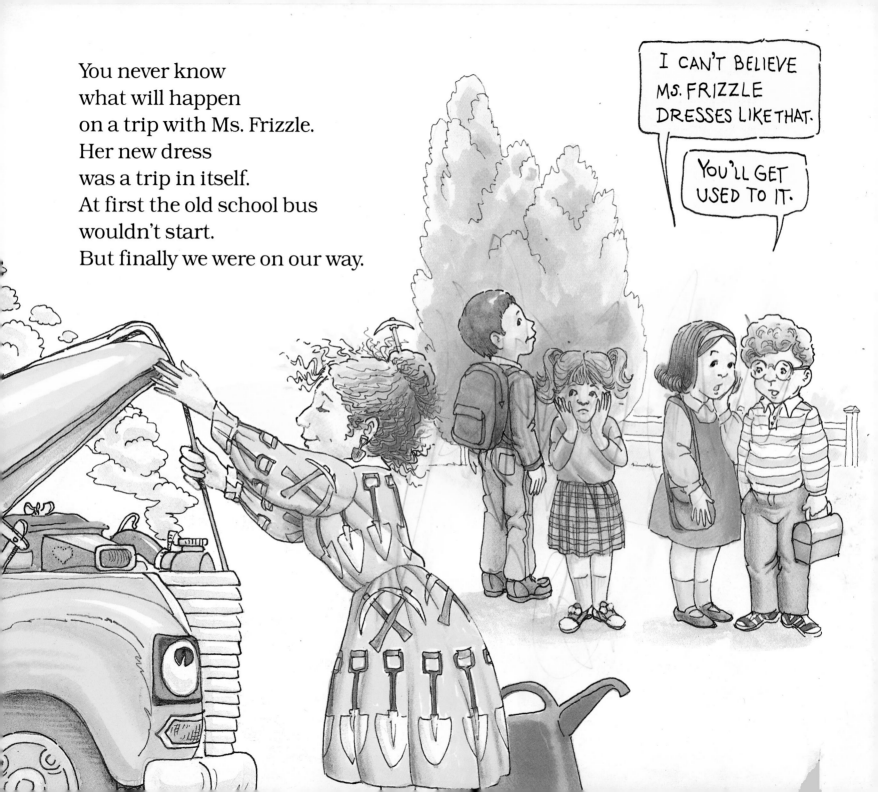

When we came to the field,
all the kids wanted
to get out of the bus.
But suddenly,
the bus began to spin like a top.
That sort of thing doesn't happen
on most class trips.

13

When the spinning finally stopped,
some things had changed.
We all had on new clothes.
The bus had turned into
a steam shovel.
And there were shovels and picks
for every kid in the class.
"Start digging!"
yelled Ms. Frizzle.
And we began making a huge hole
right in the middle of the field.

15

We chipped off pieces of the rocks
for our class rock collection.
"These rocks are called
sedimentary rocks, class,"
said Ms. Frizzle.
"There are often fossils
in sedimentary rocks."

SANDSTONE IS MADE OF GRAINS OF SAND ALL PRESSED TOGETHER.

SHALE IS MADE OF MUD AND CLAY ALL PRESSED TOGETHER.

SANDSTONE FEELS GRAINY.

THIS SHALE HAS A FOSSIL OF A LEAF IN IT.

Wouldn't you know it?
Just when we were finding
lots of fossils,
Ms. Frizzle said,
"Back on the bus, kids."
Then, as we were driving along,
we heard rock crumbling underneath us.
Down we went.
Everything was pitch black.
And we were falling, falling, falling!

We landed with a bump.
Ms. Frizzle switched on the headlights.
We had fallen through a hole
into a huge limestone cave.
"Rain water has been dripping down
through the earth for ages,"
said Ms. Frizzle.
"The water wore away this cave
in the rock."

THIS WHOLE CAVE IS MADE OF LIMESTONE. CAN YOU FIND MORE FOSSILS HERE?

HERE'S ONE, MS. FRIZZLE.

KNOCK IT OFF!

THE EMPIRE STATE BUILDING IS MADE OF LIMESTONE, TOO.

22

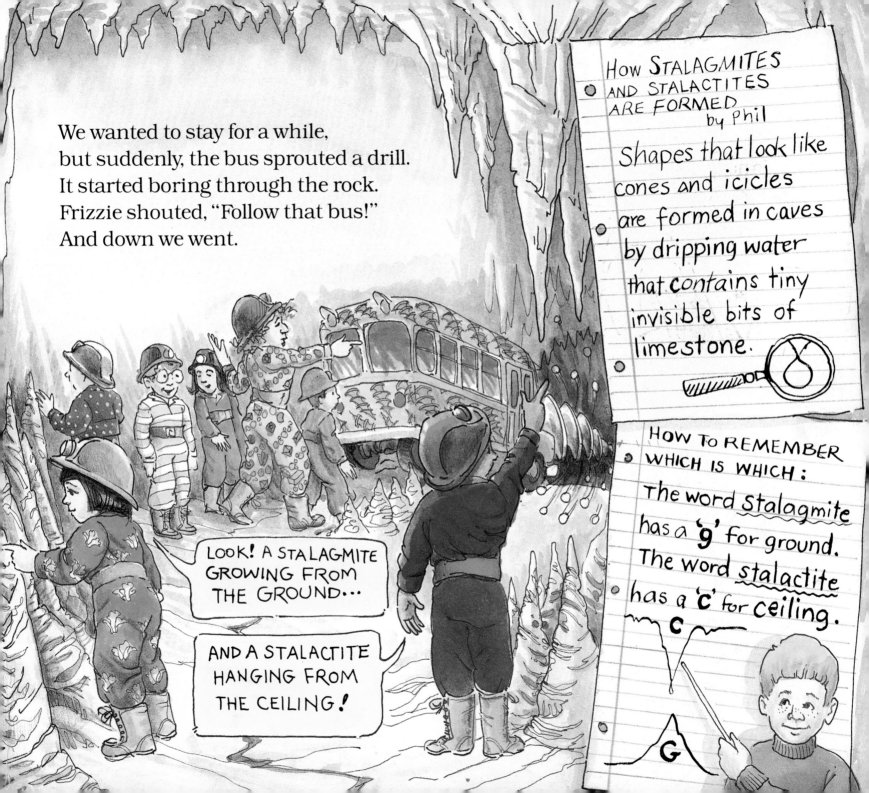

We wanted to stay for a while,
but suddenly, the bus sprouted a drill.
It started boring through the rock.
Frizzie shouted, "Follow that bus!"
And down we went.

How STALAGMITES AND STALACTITES ARE FORMED
by Phil

Shapes that look like cones and icicles are formed in caves by dripping water that contains tiny invisible bits of limestone.

LOOK! A STALAGMITE GROWING FROM THE GROUND...

AND A STALACTITE HANGING FROM THE CEILING!

HOW TO REMEMBER WHICH IS WHICH:
The word stalagmite has a 'g' for ground.
The word stalactite has a 'c' for ceiling.

We had dug all the way
through the earth's crust.
It was so hot now
that Ms. Frizzle told us to
get back in the bus.

She stepped on the gas,
and the bus started *really* drilling.
Soon we were actually inside the earth.
It was hot, hot, hot!
And it got hotter and hotter
as we zoomed toward the center.

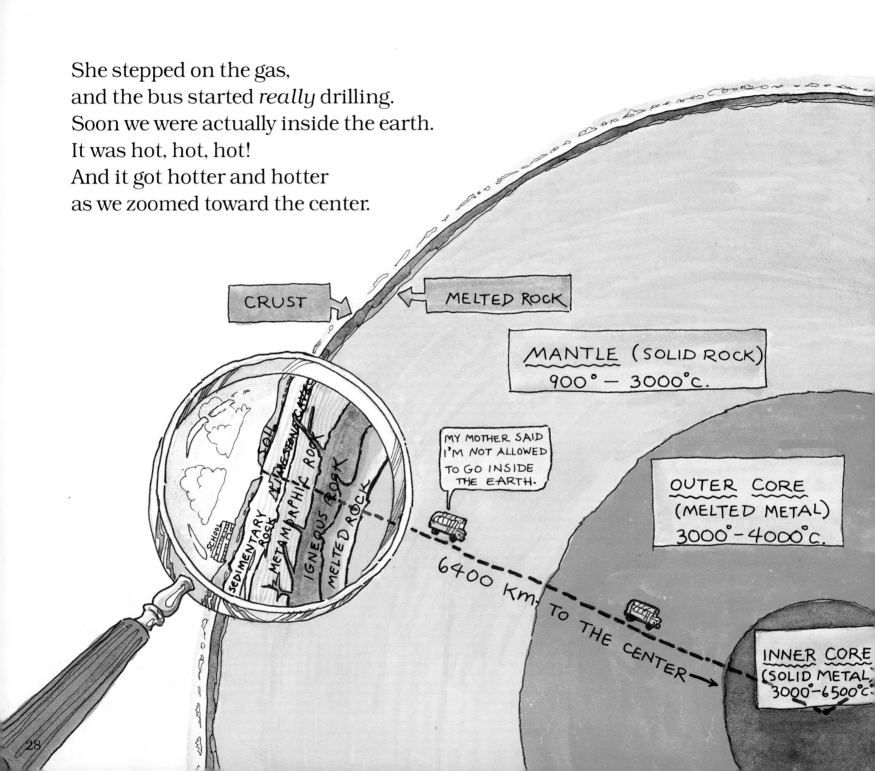

CRUST

MELTED ROCK

MANTLE (SOLID ROCK)
900° – 3000°c.

MY MOTHER SAID
I'M NOT ALLOWED
TO GO INSIDE
THE EARTH.

OUTER CORE
(MELTED METAL)
3000°- 4000°c.

6400 Km. TO THE CENTER

INNER CORE
(SOLID METAL
3000°- 6500°c.

SOIL

SEDIMENTARY ROCK

LIMESTONE CAVE

METAMORPHIC ROCK

IGNEOUS ROCK

MELTED ROCK

SCHOOL

We were glad when Ms. Frizzle
headed out again.
We reached the earth's crust
and drove straight up through
a tunnel of black rock.
It was great to see the sky.

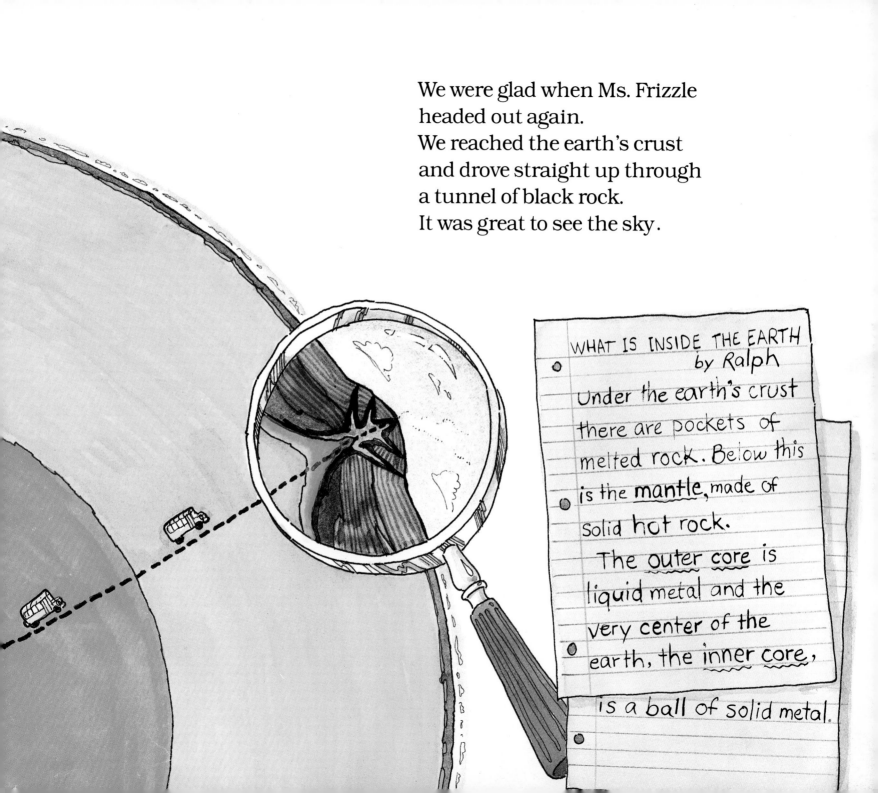

WHAT IS INSIDE THE EARTH
by Ralph

Under the earth's crust
there are pockets of
melted rock. Below this
is the <u>mantle</u>, made of
solid hot rock.
    The <u>outer core</u> is
liquid metal and the
very center of the
earth, the <u>inner core</u>,
is a ball of solid metal.

Then we looked around.
We had come out on an island
in the middle of the ocean!
"Isn't this wonderful, class?"
said Frizzie.
"We've driven right up
on a volcanic island!"
It didn't look like much.
But if Ms. Frizzle was right,
the whole island was one big volcano!

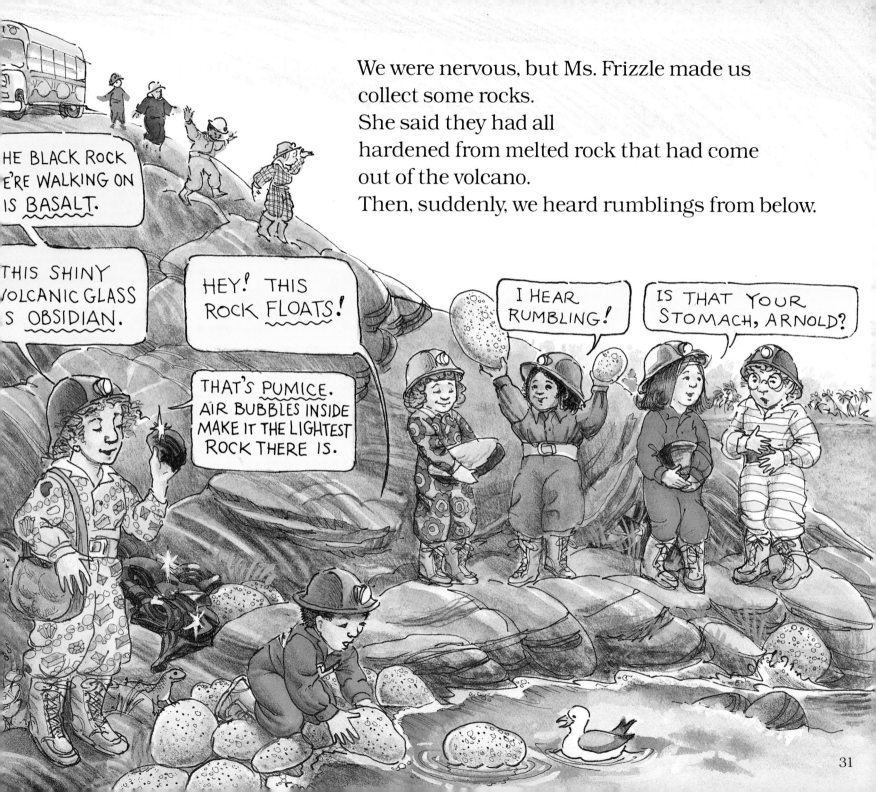

We were nervous, but Ms. Frizzle made us collect some rocks.
She said they had all hardened from melted rock that had come out of the volcano.
Then, suddenly, we heard rumblings from below.

31

VOLCANOES MAKE
NEW LAND   by Arnold

The material that comes
out of a volcano is
melted rock called lava.
When lava cools, it
hardens into new rock,
   In time, soil forms
on the rock and plants
can grow.

I DIDN'T KNOW
VOLCANOES
COULD BE USEFUL!

We scrambled into the bus.
The Friz turned the ignition key
and stepped on the gas.
Nothing happened.
The bus would not start!
We thought we were goners!

UH-OH

Red-hot lava came streaming
out of the volcano.
Some of it shot into the air
like a fountain.
Some of it flowed over the land
like a river.
Our bus went along with it—
right into the sea.

CLASS, WHEN THIS LAVA HARDENS,
IT WILL BE THE NEWEST ROCK
ON EARTH.

WHO CARES?
JUST GET US
OUT OF HERE!

When the red-hot lava hit the water,
it made a huge cloud of steam.
All we could see was white.
We seemed to be rising
with the steam and floating along.
No one knows how long
we floated in the cloud…

WHERE ARE WE?

I DON'T KNOW,
BUT I HAVE TO BE
HOME BY 3:30.

but when it finally cleared,
we were back in the school parking lot.

It had been a weird trip,
but we *did* get
a great rock collection
for our classroom.

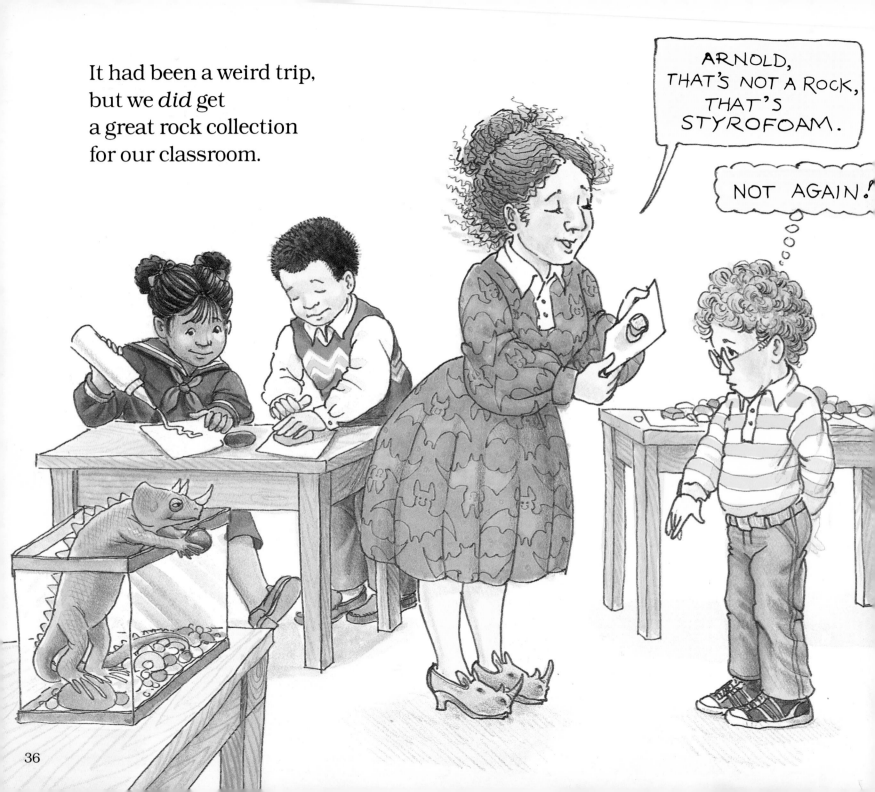

36

Rock COLLECTION
by MS. FRIZZLE'S CLASS

**HEY!
THAT'S NOT
A ROCK!**

SHIRLEY'S ROCK
LIMESTONE

TYPE: Sedimentary
(formed from shells)
USES: Buildings,
chalk, cement,
fertilizer

Amanda Jane's rock
MARBLE

TYPE: Metamorphic
(formed from limestone)
USES: Statues,
monuments, buildings

Phoebe's rock
SHALE

TYPE: Sedimentary
(formed by mud)
USES: Ground up and
mixed with limestone
for cement, brick

Wanda's rock
GRANITE

TYPE: Igneous
USES: Monuments,
buildings, curbstones

JOHN'S rock
SLATE

TYPE: Metamorphic
(formed from shale)
USES: Roofing tile,
flagstones, chalkboards

Michael's rock
SANDSTONE

TYPE: Sedimentary
(formed by sand)
USES: Buildings,
grindstones

MOLLY'S rock
BASALT

TYPE: Igneous
(volcanic)
USES: Road Building

Rachel's rock
OBSIDIAN

TYPE: Igneous
(volcanic)
USES: Decoration,
Indian Arrowheads

Florrie's rock
PUMICE

TYPE: Igneous
(volcanic)
USES: Ground-up in
scouring powder

Phil's rock
QUARTZITE

TYPE: Metamorphic
(formed from
sandstone)
USES: Millstones for
grinding grain,
road building

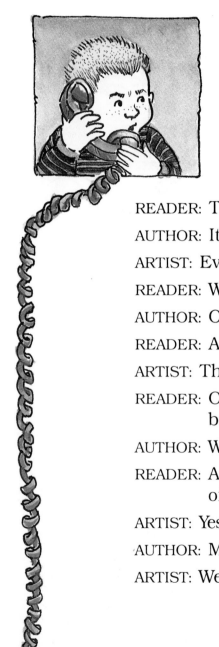

A WORD WITH THE AUTHOR AND THE ARTIST

The first reader of this book called to complain. He said the book was full of mistakes. We recorded the conversation to help you decide which things are true and which were put in to make the story more exciting.

READER: This book is full of mistakes!

AUTHOR: It is not!

ARTIST: Everything in this book is absolutely true and really happened.

READER: What about the beaver lodge on page 7?

AUTHOR: Oh, that. Well, I guess that *would* be too messy in a real classroom.

READER: And the beehive?

ARTIST: That, too. But everything else is fact.

READER: Oh, come *on!* You mean kids can use jackhammers (page 16), and a bus can change into a steam shovel (page 14) and a drill (page 23)?

AUTHOR: Well, er, now that you mention it, that is not really possible.

READER: And do you expect me to believe that a bus can go through the center of the earth (page 28)?

ARTIST: Yes....

AUTHOR: Maybe....

ARTIST: Well, actually, no. The bus couldn't do that, either.

AUTHOR: Even if a bus *could* drill its way through, the distance is so long that the trip would take months, even years.

READER: And what about the heat?

AUTHOR: Okay, okay! It's white-hot in the center of the earth. The bus would be burned up in a minute.

READER: Isn't it kind of ridiculous to say that air-conditioning would help?

AUTHOR: Gee, you're a tough cookie! Okay, you're right. Air-conditioning could not make any difference in that kind of heat.

READER: And the bus could not flow in lava and go up in a cloud of steam (pages 33-34)?

ARTIST: Give us a break! You're right again. That's not true, either.

READER: But you said *everything* was true!

AUTHOR: Everything *else* is. Honest!

READER: Everything else is true? There truly are sedimentary, metamorphic, and igneous rocks?

AUTHOR: Certainly!

READER: And lava really does harden into new rock?

ARTIST: Oh, yes.

READER: And what about Ms. Frizzle's clothing?

AUTHOR: That *is* hard to believe, but it's true.

ARTIST: She really does dress that way!

HOW TO SAY OUR NEW EARTH SCIENCE WORDS

basalt
(buh·SAWLT)

granite
(GRAN·it)

igneous
(IHG·nee·uhs)

lava
(LAH·vuh)

metamorphic
(met·uh·MAWR·fik)

obsidian
(ahb·SIHD·ee·un)

pumice
(PUHM·ihs)

quartzite
(KWAWRT·site)

sedimentary
(sed·uh·MEN·tar·ee)

stalactite
(stuh·LAK·tite)

stalagmite
(stuh·LAG·mite)